This book
belongs to:

Mom Has Cancer!

Text: *Jennifer Moore-Mallinos*

Illustrations: *Marta Fàbrega*

BARRON'S

Ever since last week a lot of things have changed, and I don't know why! Mom and Dad don't laugh and joke around like they used to, and often leave to go to another appointment with the doctor. Then, when they get home, they're really quiet and look very sad. I'm a bit scared.

4-5

Maybe I did something wrong and they're mad at
me. I keep forgetting to make my bed before I
go to school or perhaps they got a phone call from
my teacher about the test we had the other day; it
was really hard and I didn't do so well. I just wish I
knew what was going on ... then maybe I'd be able to
help make things better again.

Today when I got home from school and Mom and Dad were waiting for me in the kitchen, that's when I knew that something must have happened. First, Mom made sure that I knew that I hadn't done anything wrong, and then she said that she needed to talk to me about something very important.

I sat down at the kitchen table and Mom told me that the doctor found a cancerous tumor inside her. That means that a part of her body is sick and the doctor will try to cure it. At first I was scared, because I knew that having cancer wasn't good and I didn't want anything bad to happen to Mom.

Mom also told me that she will have to go to the hospital every week for chemotherapy. That's a special medicine that will help get rid of  Mom's cancer but, because it is a very strong medicine, it will make her really sick and she'll probably lose all of her hair.

Dad told me that he and I will help Mom get better. We agreed that I will continue doing all the things that I always do, like keeping my room clean and doing my homework.

Dad said that some things will change around
the house, but most things will stay the same.
I will have to go to school every day, and
even if Mom won't be able to come to
my soccer practices or games, she'll be
home waiting for me to come back.

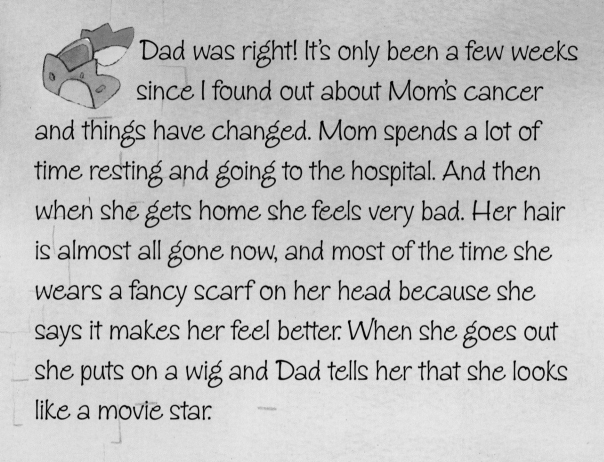 Dad was right! It's only been a few weeks since I found out about Mom's cancer and things have changed. Mom spends a lot of time resting and going to the hospital. And then when she gets home she feels very bad. Her hair is almost all gone now, and most of the time she wears a fancy scarf on her head because she says it makes her feel better. When she goes out she puts on a wig and Dad tells her that she looks like a movie star.

I try to help Mom by not making too much noise while she's resting, and when she's sick I bring her a glass of water and a cold cloth to put on her forehead. Mom really likes it when I climb up into her bed and we look at a book together or play a game of cards. Mom says spending time with me is the best medicine in the world.

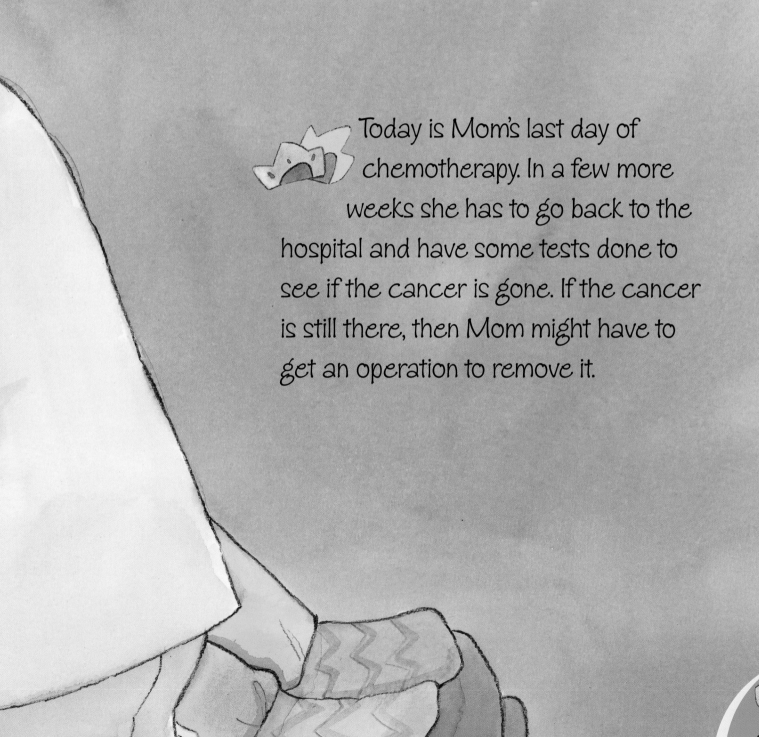

Today is Mom's last day of chemotherapy. In a few more weeks she has to go back to the hospital and have some tests done to see if the cancer is gone. If the cancer is still there, then Mom might have to get an operation to remove it.

Good news! Mom's cancer is all gone, so that means that for the time being she's OK. Mom told me that she will have to keep going to see the doctor every few months to make sure that the cancer hasn't come back.

Mom's hair is growing back and she's starting to feel a lot better. She's even teased Dad about his awful cooking! I didn't know how much I missed having Mom at my soccer games until today, when she was there sitting on the bench and cheering me on like she used to. And when I scored a goal, she was the one I could hear cheering the most!

Cancer was bad for everybody.
Dad and I didn't have cancer, but
it was really hard for us, too. We
were very sad seeing Mom so
sick, and when she
didn't have any hair it
kept reminding us that she had
cancer. But now that Mom is
better, things are going back to
the way they used to be, except
now we spend way more time
together and that's just great!

Note to adults

There are many families confronted with the harsh reality of a diagnosis of cancer. Although such a crisis impacts all members of a family, it is children who usually have a more difficult time in coping with the situation.

Being diagnosed with cancer is perhaps one of the most difficult things for any individual and his or her family members to face. The high level of uncertainly that accompanies a diagnosis of cancer can be overwhelming for everybody, including children.

As parents, we instinctively want to shield our children from many of the realities of life and, as a result, our first response to bad news often is an attempt to hide them. However, despite our good intentions, this may not always turn out to be the best policy in the long run because, eventually, they are going to learn the truth and wonder why you weren't up front with them.

Children can be very perceptive and be able to sense when something is wrong or when something doesn't feel right, and they are very good at recognizing when something around them changes. For example, they may notice a change of dynamics between their parents because they look sad and are not as talkative, or perhaps they notice a change in their daily routine as a result of the stress caused by the diagnosis. All of these things that children observe and feel can create additional stress and feelings of helplessness because they simply don't know the reason.

Just like adults, children need to have answers. And when there are no answers made available to them, they will often search for one by creating possible reasons as to what could be happening around them. Children's fear of the unknown may in fact be creating additional stress when they start inventing answers for what they are feeling.

Mom Has Cancer! takes the perspective that it's better for children to know when a parent is diagnosed with cancer. Children are going to be frightened when they learn that their mother or father has cancer, but not knowing about it can end up being a lot worse. Once children are aware of a parent's diagnosis, it's important to reassure them that cancer is not contagious and that cancer is not a result of something they did. Children may also worry that anybody who gets cancer will die. This might be a good time to explain to them that there have been many medical advances in cancer research, detection, and treatment and, as a result, the outcome is much more hopeful than it was in the past.

MOM HAS CANCER!

First edition for the United States and
Canada published in 2008 by Barron's Educational Series, Inc.
© Copyright 2008 by Gemser Publications, S.L.
C/Castell, 38; Teià (08329), Barcelona, Spain (World Rights)
Author: Jennifer Moore-Mallinos
Illustrator: Marta Fàbrega

All inquiries should be addressed to:
Barron's Educational Series, Inc.
250 Wireless Boulevard
Hauppauge, NY 11788
www.barronseduc.com

ISBN-13: 978-0-7641-4074-7
ISBN-10: 0-7641-4074-4

Library of Congress Control Number: 2008926679

Printed in China
9 8 7 6 5 4 3 2 1